Books by Cheryl Lafferty Eckl

Personal Growth & Transformation

A Beautiful Death:
Keeping the Promise of Love

A Beautiful Grief:
Reflections on Letting Go

The LIGHT Process:
Living on the Razor's Edge of Change

Wise Inner Counselor Books
Reflections on Being Your True Self in Any Situation
Reflections on Doing Your Great Work in Any Occupation
Reflections on Ineffable Love: from loss through grief to joy

Poetry for Inspiration & Beauty

Poetics of Soul & Fire

Bridge to the Otherworld

Idylls from the Garden of Spiritual Delights & Healing

Sparks of Celtic Mystery:
soul poems from Éire

A Beautiful Joy: Reunion with the Beloved
Through Transfiguring Love

Twin Flames Romance Novels

The Weaving:
A Novel of Twin Flames Through Time

Twin Flames of Éire Trilogy
The Ancients and The Call
The Water and The Flame
The Mystics and The Mystery

A Beautiful Joy

Reunion with the Beloved
Through Transfiguring Love

Cheryl Lafferty Eckl
with Stephen Alan Eckl

FLYING CRANE PRESS

A BEAUTIFUL JOY: REUNION WITH THE BELOVED
THROUGH TRANSFIGURING LOVE
© 2019, 2021, 2022 Cheryl J. Eckl, LLC

Published by Flying Crane Press, Livingston, Montana 59047
Cheryl@CherylEckl.com | www.CherylEckl.com

All poems and epigraphs are © 2016-2019

Select images and art not the author's own are used by permission of the artist or photographer; or are free stock images from pixabay.com, or from NASA.gov Hubble image gallery; NASA.gov/GSFC; or are royalty-free purchases of standard permitted use images through 123rf.com, dreamstime.com; bigstockphoto.com.

All rights reserved. No part of this book may be used, reproduced, translated, electronically stored, or transmitted in any manner whatsoever without prior written permission from the author or publisher, except by reviewers, who may quote brief text only passages in their reviews.

Library of Congress Control Number: 2019904002
ISBN: 978-0-9970376-9-2 (paperback)
ISBN: 978-0-9970376-8-5 (e-book)

Printed in the United States of America

*To all who yearn
for the Beloved*

Contents

Sharing the Joy We Found

Our Journey through Transfiguring Love	4
An Invitation from the Spirit of Love	10
A Beautiful Joy	13
A Beginning	14

Embracing the Deep Work of Liberating a Soul

A Soul's Prayer to the Spirit of Love	19
Life Can Be	21
Treasures Born of Spirit's Presence	23
A Prayer for Deliverance	26
Love Speaks	29
A Soul's Admonition to a Friend	32
Coming Out of Silence	34
A Vivid Step	36
Returning	38
Stepping through the Veil	40

Learning to Dance on the Bridge Between Worlds

Crossing Over from Earth	45
Galaxies	49

A Million Ways	52
Equinox	54
Helping	57
All in a Day	58
Love of My Life	60
The Presence	62
When Grief Departs	65
Linked by a Silver Thread	68

Communing in the Ecstasy of Love Unbounded

Sacred Embrace	73
Love's Persons	74
Contact	77
Recollection	78
We Will Always Have Roses	80
Duet	82
Surrounded in Love	85
The Meeting Place	86
A Blanket of Comfort for the Soul	88
These Days, Celebrate	89
Return to Innocence	90

Living Life to the Full

A Promise	95
What We Do for Love	97
My Brother	99
Acknowledging What Is	101
At Home in Love's Garden	102
Lean on Faith	104
Hope's Gift of Renewal	106
Love in Action	109
Life Lived to the Full	110
Grounded in Glory	111
The Heart of the Matter	112

Sparkling Like Diamonds

The Best Days of Our Lives	117
Antiphon of Rejoicing	119
In an Orb of Love's Pure Radiance	122

The Key that Opens the Door

Accepting the Gift of Transfiguration	129
Our Hearts Overflow with Gratitude	131

Welcome to our sanctuary.
We have prepared a feast for you.
Please, come & dine.

*May you be blessed
with the embrace of oneness
that was yours in the beginning.*

Our Journey through Transfiguring Love
Hearth-fires burn brightly in honor of your visit

Here in the sanctuary of the heart, Love beckons.
Love illumines. Love strengthens.
Love initiates us into its deep mysteries.
Love changes our world when we least expect it.
And, when we allow, Love transfigures us into who
we really are—the radiant twin of our soul's other half.

Cheryl's Welcome - Accepting Love's Invitation

My husband, Stephen, and I accepted Love's invitation and stepped into a future that was more like picking up from another lifetime than beginning a new adventure in this one.

The life that Love gave us has become a sacred journey in the years since my darling took off for other worlds—fueled by his desire for union with his own inner divinity and by his determination to comfort me from the Beyond in his apparent absence from this earth.

Stephen walks beside me in spirit—supporting, encouraging, sometimes admonishing—always leading me closer to reunion with his spirit as my soul's beloved twin flame, and with my True Self: the Beloved with a capital "B."

When we are most attuned to the promptings of that True Self, our conversations are joined by the Spirit of Love, who speaks into our hearts as a wise and vivid presence.

Our Path as Twin Flames

In the beginning of our relationship, we set an intention to overcome negative patterns of thought, feeling and behavior as part of our desire for true reunion. Immediately Love began to transform us in an alchemy that unfolded as spirals of self-transcendence.

These frequent episodes of spiritual quickening intensified during Stephen's illness and after his passing. In each instance, our connection was so electric that I felt myself changed, elevated to a more profound bonding with my True Self and with Stephen's spirit. I have also gained deeper understanding of our mission as twin flames—two souls created as one in the beginning.

Stephen and I intuitively knew we were one another's twin soul. Our personalities were very different, but our essence was the same. We were so complete in each other that we honestly forgot to need anyone else. Then very early one morning, my beloved went on to spiritual realms, where he remains vitally alive.

Although we had time to prepare for his departure from this earth, nothing ever really primes you for the stunning absence of your spouse, especially when that one is your twin flame. To me, the experience was like losing half of my heart, for Stephen took it with him. I have since come to realize that he left me half of his.

We Have Been Changed in Love's Alchemy

Gradually, as our soul communication became more facile, our love that was precious in physical life became luminous in the spiritual collaboration that remains for us more real than touch, more intimate than a kiss, more transformative than the most tender physical lovemaking. Our hearts now beat as one in two worlds.

We have been changed in Love's alchemy—transfigured into equal partners who dance together, sublimely unified, back and forth across the veil between spirit and matter.

Of course, there continues to be labor here for both of us. Yet, in our fervent desire for oneness with our own inner divinity, the voice of our soul's other half echoes in the voice of Love's Spirit, who sweeps us up to planes of ineffable joy where we feel the wholeness of our beings—as above, so below.

The Gift of Joy We Are Delighted to Share

I listen without ceasing for the intimations that often sail in unannounced from my beloved. I treasure his presence. I feel his thoughts press in on mine as guidance or inspiration. He frequently speaks to me in verse and I write back—just as we did while he was physically present.

Occasionally, he will urge me to go on an adventure where poems and stories emerge as shared experience. When I am quiet, I feel our hearts conjoin in Love's Spirit that leads us to our ultimate goal of union with the Divine Presence who is the All-in-all.

We are delighted to share with you this work that has emerged from the very depths of our souls. May you bask in your own cosmic sojourn with transfiguring Love all the days of your life. And may these conversations between worlds bring you comfort and hope that what one pair of twin flames has done, others can do.

Oh, that I could bring you to where I am!
To show you the exquisite beauty of this heaven world.
To walk with you through ethereal gardens
fragrant with roses, gardenias, lilacs and jasmine.
To take you with me to crystalline halls of learning.
To fly with you among the stars that sing of pure joy.

Stephen's Welcome - **The Story I Wish to Tell**

As I neared the end of my life, I knew my body was fading. I believed my soul would live on; however, I did not want to come back in another round on the wheel of life. I also wanted Cheryl to transcend the need for re-embodiment at the end of her current earthly sojourn.

I chose to keep going in the physical for as long as possible. I worked hard on my spiritual life, creating a magnet of Light energy in my chakras through prayer and meditation, so that Spirit could pull my soul up to etheric octaves when my body expired.

Cheryl and I also worked to unite our consciousness with each other, with our True Self and with the Spirit of Love. Through the connection we achieved, she heard me call her name in my final hour as my body lay in a coma. She heard me the morning after my passing when I exclaimed in ecstasy, "There is joy in heaven!" She hears me now, for my voice has become congruent with hers.

Our Communion Has Been Dearly Won

After departing this earth, I was grateful to arrive in the realms of Light I had expected to find. What surprised me was my ability to reach out to my sweetheart who remained in the physical, even as I continued my soul journey in the etheric.

I thought I would have remembered that gift from previous transitions, but for some reason I did not. There is much we do not recall until we are fully integrated into life here on the Other Side.

Sadly, as I neared my transition, I had told Cheryl not to try to find me—that I would be long gone into higher octaves. Instead, I could stand right next to her, though she could not see me. For several months, she suffered through conflicting thoughts and feelings, doing her best to believe what I had said, despite having a strong sense of my presence.

We Are More Connected Than We Know

My observation is that—at least for a time after their passing—many newly departed souls are able to contact their loved ones in the physical, if only they would listen. But this connection is not taught and is not encouraged, leaving many to suffer needlessly a sense of separation that is not real.

There are a few who understand. A woman who participated in a weekend retreat that Cheryl conducted on transforming grief explained that her late husband had brought the program to her attention in their own conversations between worlds. But this was an exception.

Other recently deceased souls I met here in the etheric were most often disappointed because their loved ones who were still in embodiment either could not or would not accept the possibility of communication and soul growth after a person has crossed over to the Other Side.

Of course, we do not demand connection after death. But for those who are twin flames, the contact can be sustained for many years as they continue their ongoing mission with one on each side of the veil between worlds.

Now I understand—the key is for partners and family members, twin flames in particular, to discover and practice the form of their most intimate soul conversation while they both live in a body. Without realizing it, that is what Cheryl and I did through poetry.

Our Poetical Connection
We must have been bards in previous lifetimes because we are poets to the core. From the first days of our marriage, we gravitated to verse as our favorite art form.

Some of our deepest soul connections came through reading poems to each other. As I approached my life's end, writing poetry became our way of sharing thoughts and feelings that were too tender for normal conversation.

These days, the verses we compose bring us closer to each other and to the Spirit of Love that sustains us in the quiet place where we commune together. Each day we discover more deeply how indelible our oneness has become and how it grows even stronger when we let Love lead the way.

Not All Twin Flames Are Spouses
Cheryl and I were fortunate to be together in this life as husband and wife. We do not take this opportunity for granted because many twin flames are not alive at the same time, in the same place or in a romantic relationship.

However, I have observed here in the etheric that their soul connection usually remains intact at inner levels. I have also noticed that many twin flames strengthen their bond by treating any close human relationship as if that person were their soul's twin.

Where We Are Today
Cheryl has often said that I was her teacher, though she was and is equally mine. In our marriage she was my perfect complement: extrovert to my introvert; animated to my passion for an economy of motion.

Still, there was much we did not understand about each other during our time together on earth. These days we continue to learn and extend the forgiveness that is sometimes hard to come by in the midst of our physical lives as imperfect human beings.

From my perspective here in a realm that is not subject to the limitations of time and space, I can support and intensify Cheryl's spiritual progress, offering her encouragement and providing her with insight into our souls' remaining obligations in service to life.

She continues as our hands and feet, doing for both of us the work on earth that we could not accomplish while I was still in a physical body—either because we ran out of time or because neither of us was ready for the intimate disclosure of our spiritual path that we are now offering from our hearts to yours.

Fulfilling an Ancient Goal
The goal of our many lifetimes has been the reunion of our twin flames. We are profoundly grateful to the great Wisdom Teachers who have given us the opportunity in this life to experience that sublime reality and to share with you the beautiful joy we have found in our journey through transfiguring Love.

An Invitation from the Spirit of Love
Love greets you with open arms

Step into your heart, dear one,
and rise with me
into the holy of holies,
the secret chamber,
which is my Home.

I speak as the voice
of your True Self,
one with the Divine,
embodied and ensconced forever
in the purest center of your being.

I would commune with you in peace.

For peace opens the way to Joy,
as she steps in lightly
when your world is free
of strife or struggle
or harsh words.

Joyful giving produces peace;
you see, they dance together.

Close your eyes now
and breathe with me,
easily in tender calm.

There is no need to take a breath
when breath is given and received,

a delicate interchange of peace,
a subtle infusion
of profound wisdom
that seeps in,
gently pervading your whole being,
comforting as a downy robe.

Feel the sense of inner peace
increase its centered fire
in your breast.

We are deep within the Self,
in a space as vast as a galaxy,
as intimate as a single breath,
a cave of light, perhaps,
whose crystalline walls
reflect the virtues
of Love's truth,
where peace brings balance
to the flame.

As the feeling of peace increases
we enter a familiar garden
fragrant with roses, lilies
and orange blossoms.

Gardenias and myriad
tropical flowers honey the air
as Light suffuses the atmosphere

like new dawn's rays
of golden pink
and violet hues.

Here is the peace
I hope for you
in faith that all
your selfless striving
will bear sweet fruit
in abundant gifts
of tender communion
that come to you
on wings of joy.

Peace does not hurry
and all important work
is done.

A Beautiful Joy
She muses from the physical realm

A beautiful joy occurs
    when the Divine is present,
    when worlds are joined
    across a bridge of unselfish love;
    holiness is its flavor
    and mercy its expression.

Tears come—
    not from sadness,
    though loss may be the impetus;
    but more from recognition
    that this is what Home feels like:

        the utter acceptance
        of one's being
        of one's gifts
        even of one's failings
        and of one's longing
        to be more of that—

            that openness
            that givingness
            that tenderness
            that fullness
            that indescribable
                  something

    that knits up hearts
    in unity and care,
    making all unlike itself pale
    and fall away, as if nothing less
    than pure love ever happened.

A Beginning
He speaks from the etheric realm

I am a spirit now
    and not a man,
    though I was a man once
    or thrice or a thousand times before.

So I speak as incorporeal
    about the things of earth—
    of human love and loss
    of work and play
    of failure and success
    of being and doing
    of living life to the full
    and drinking deeply of sorrow's cup
    over leaving behind
    all I had come to cherish
    more earnestly than life itself.

And finally of transfiguration,
    as all my strivings were transformed
    into the ecstasy of love unbounded;
    of twin hearts linked by a silver thread
    grown stronger in mutual devotion
    while learning to dance upon the bridge
    'twixt our two worlds,
    until reunion should call me
    to speak my peace;
    for peace it is and perfect joy
    that are the substance of my life.

This is the story I wish to tell,
    which surprises me
    that I should ever disclose,
    even from this imaginal realm,
    the secret self I kept tucked away
    from all but my beloved.

Yet, this is service,
    as I came to see
    when life broke my heart
    and I flew off to other worlds;
    now to return,
    joined with my sweetheart,
    one in an orb of love's pure radiance,
    sublimely able at last
    to reveal the journey of my soul
    from darkness into light, or better said,
    from ignorance to illumination,
    to the joy of perfect unity
    that sparkles like diamonds
    or tears of recognition in my lover's eyes.

I speak because she listens
    and knows my voice—
    sometimes better than her own

Come, join us now, attend with your full being
and witness what reunion can accomplish.

Embracing the Deep Work of Liberating a Soul

*With generous help from Spirit,
twin flames who are still
in physical embodiment
strive to transcend
their human imperfections.*

*May your path lead you always
in the intimate awareness
that you live in the palm
of a divine hand.*

A Soul's Prayer to the Spirit of Love
The embodied soul strives for spiritual attunement

O Essence of Love!
Speak to me of longing,
of yearning to feel
the fervent substance
of your spirit-flame
kindled in my heart,
consuming all lesser loves,
taking me apart
then, piece by piece,
reconstructing my mind,
my will, my being
in the image of your Self.

How is it possible to live
in this world as me, as you,
as true to Love's highest
and most tender aspects?

Only in the miracle of your Presence
do I feel myself alive and worthy
to speak of Love's delicacy
or its power to remove mountains
of human willfulness.

My ignorance astounds me
while walking in the desert
of lovelessness on days
when I do not feel you here,
sparking the inner fire
I have come to rely upon.

What about me causes you
to come and go?

These are secrets I long to learn;
yet, in saying so,
an insight sails into my mind
as if a wise spirit had answered me:

Love's Spirit speaks
>Your soul already knows
its origin and its destiny.

Still your worried thoughts
and feel the rhythm
of surrender's purest alchemy
that unlocks Love's deepest mysteries.

All knowledge abides
in the heart's inner chamber,
where mind knows its place
as guard at the door
so nothing may disturb
beloveds in their loving.

Life Can Be
Insights from Love's Spirit

Your fear wants your love.

All those disowned portions of self
    want to come home,
      to be gathered into your embrace
      like prodigal sons and daughters
      who long to receive again
      their parents' acceptance.

You are father, mother, daughter, son:
    worthy in all aspects.

Accept yourself as my Spirit does;
    and learn once again
    that all is Love and only Love,
    which you contain
    and are contained within
    as lover and Beloved True Self.

Be that cherished one
    and fear will not trouble you,
    for you will have welcomed it
    home for healing.

Bounce back, no matter
    the grievances thrust upon
    your character's impeccability.

Those who aim for the heights
> are bound to suffer thunderclaps
> and rumblings from lesser gods
> only skilled at hurling boulders.

The path narrows near the summit;
> watch your step
> like a seasoned climber
> and be not distracted by
> subtle conundrums
> from wily minds.

Ours is the mystic way
> known of old to pilgrims
> who do not mind
> a few pebbles in their boots.

Embrace your fears
> and learn what life can be.

Treasures Born of Spirit's Presence
The soul hears the voice of the Beloved True Self

>Silence. Space. Solitude.
>The quiet grace
>of contemplation
>and the privacy to mourn
>the soul's acute grief
>over separation
>from her Divine Source,
>causing her to yearn
>and grow more ready
>for reconciliation.
>
>In this loneliness
>communion arises;
>in this soundless chamber
>a wise inner voice is heard.

THE BELOVED SPEAKS
>Listen well, dear soul.
>Create honest hospitality
>and open all the gateways
>of your inner knowing
>so that blessedness
>may glide in on angel wings
>of meditation's sanctity.
>
>Gather lilies made of starlight;
>cherish every good and thoughtful
>word or deed.

These are treasures
born of Spirit's Presence,
meant to be borne
as you would
carry a pack for hiking.

See how, with every
compassionate act,
your burden
grows more light.

Till light upon light
dissolves the weight,
leaving only
paradigms of holiness,

the luminance of Spirit
that pulls the soul
Home to her True Self,

the perfect magnet
for a final step
toward the liberating ecstasy
of Love's sweet reunion.

A Prayer for Deliverance
A soul seeks acceleration on the path of reunion

Give me my dark nights.
Let me be broken on the wheel of loss,
Stripped of reason and safety,
Fed to the beasts of pride.

May I suffer the injustice of human treachery,
And taste the bile of disappointed dreams.

When hope flees and despair howls
In the depths of my brokenness,
Then, and only then,
Will I be clay malleable enough
For the Potter's hand.

I would earn this annihilation;
Though it catch me by surprise,
Arriving in the stead of accolades
Expected by an ego basking
In the world's acclaim.

My striving wearies me.
Why do I try to make roses bloom?
Only faith and sacrifice
Can free my soul to be her perfect Self.

In darkness are we born,
So I seek the void
Whose mysteries cannot be known
In seeking or in thought.

O, my Beloved, take me to your Self
And teach me to surrender
Strife of my own doing.

I am still afraid of the dark.
Yet all the resurrected parts of me
Call out to you for trials of moonless nights,
Dark caverns and the plunging abyss
Where Spirit's purest alchemy takes place,
And all my strivings are transformed
In the furnace of your sublime
Transfiguring fire.

Love Speaks
Encouragement from the Spirit of Love

I am the flame in your heart;
    the rose you see and feel
        in moments of deepest harmony.

I would speak to you of Love;
    Love that is alive,
    nurturing, expanding,
    blazing with life becoming
    more of Life and unified
    with every spark
    of the Divine you cherish

    until Love so permeates
    every precious person
    that you and they
    merge into my flame.

I consume all unlike myself.

My nature is to so adore,
    so extend, so burn
    with the ardor of pure being
    that I can be naught
    but what I am—

    a fire transforming
    all of life into its essence,
    which is myself.

Flow unto me
>   as I flow unto you, dear one.

Come, join in our sublime reunion;
>   for you have called
>   and I have answered,
>   bursting forth—I must!

I cannot be contained
>   once you have set your attention
>   on fire with the fullness
>   of your contemplation.

I am the substance of your divinity,
>   your soul, your very being.

I am Love—alive forever,
>   carrying you in my embrace
>   that counts not the cost
>   of surrender or of sacrifice
>   when transfiguration
>   is the prize—the goal
>   of all your journeying.

I cannot leave you
>   as I found you;
>   and that is Love's great gift.

Though the burning of myself in you
> may feel like a sharpness
> in the breast,
> stay with the flame as it expands
> and you will come to know
> joy unlimited:

> exquisite joy
> that is the atmosphere,
> the taste,
> the fragrance,
> the touch
> of my attention.

Be with me where I am
> and know yourself enkindled
> with the flame that is alive in you
> as a portion of myself.

This is the story you came to tell.

A Soul's Admonition to a Friend
Souls of both men & women speak as feminine

Do not pity me.
I am not poor or weak
in the pain of my humanness.

What you see is a soul
working out her destiny,
endeavoring to come up higher,
to reach into the invisible world
so she may blend this realm
of time and space
with what is unseen,
though profoundly felt.

Do not pity one who journeys,
who marks her life by milestones
of loving surrender—
not merely of a mulish will,
but of lesser voices
that would render her complacent
when labor is required.

For entering and leaving earth
are both arduous,
as is living all
the intervening years.

I am grateful for the effort
I have spent in striving;
I have a path to show for it.

Be glad for me and all who climb
mountains of transfiguration's alchemy.

We are happy warriors
who rejoice in our adventures.

We harbor no regrets
to spoil our arrival in that fair place
where land and sea and sky convene—
our destination that hides,
all shrouded in mist
until the final hour of our travels.

How grateful we will be
to one day walk in that finer realm
where pity is impossible
and joy the order of the day.

Coming Out of Silence
Insights from the Beloved

Each day you choose
past, present or future
by where you set your gaze.

Of course,
you only have today
for loving where you are
or longing for where you want to be.

You choose what will enliven you,
what will set your zeal aflame,
what will kindle the soul-fires
that beckon you to resurrection;
what will melt the chill of loss
that kept you frozen out of life,
no longer aware
of being in cold storage.

Cycles turn;
you lift your eyes
toward dawning fingers
of ruby, purple, orange and gold.

A full-moon day is on the rise,
and so are you.

Life is calling you at last
to emerge out of silence,
out of a stony solitude
that had forgotten how to smile,
or laugh or sing or dance or love.

Pull on your boots
and set your cap;
stride out into the morning air,
and fill your lungs
with the effervescence
of being here,
alive again.

Resist the temptation
to look back over your shoulder.

The only thing you will see
is your shadow
running to keep up
with one who races the dawn
to the top of the mountain.

A Vivid Step
Twin flames share a peak experience

We do not travel to our sacred center
as to a place or at a distance.

We are simply there
in a perpetual motion
that continuously pours itself out
as Love creating Love, singing,
"Abide with me, abide with me."

The overflowing chalice
does not perceive itself,
for there is no separate Grail Cup
standing back to say,
"Here I am and there you are."

The burning, spinning, radiating
heart in Love is all that exists.

We are subsumed in its rosy perfume;
we have dissolved
into the pure essence of the Divine
that can only be experienced
as deep inhalation
where one becomes nothing more
than a whiff of the ineffable.

A vivid step—we feel the movement now
as mind surrenders all its knowing
and sinks gratefully into deep pools
of adoration's unending embrace

where thought and feeling join
in a reborn way of perceiving
that is not seeing,
but simply resting
in mutual resonance
that knows no separation
between one and the other.

Love appears in a cloud
of opalescent radiance,
enfolding and unfolding
in deepening ecstasy
whose only limit
is the soul's capacity
to, hour by hour,
become more of her True Self

overcoming resistance to Love
through Love, in Love
while the rose of the heart opens,
petal by petal,
as each act of selflessness
purifies all unlike
the honeyed sweetness
of divine Love
until transfiguration's alchemy
precipitates the All-in-all.

O, that we could retain this vision!
"You will," says Love's Spirit. "Soon, you will."

Returning
She bids her twin soul adieu as he leaves this world

Though I weep at your departure,
yet I bless you, my darling,
as you return to your soul's Home,
your place of origin and finale.

You will find no endings there,
only new beginnings
and the Beloved's call to be more real

and profoundly passionate
in your longing
for the holy communion
that happens when your soul
nestles into peaceful repose

content in her surroundings
that buoy her reality
in the company of other pilgrims
who cherish their sojourning
at least as dearly as their destination.

Well-meaning hands
of others may cling;
but when you turn toward Home
none can hold you back
from the reunion we both know
to be your destiny.

We will meet in the middle place,
my darling.

You reaching down,
me reaching up,
both of us across and in
to the presence of the other

in the blessed contact
that knows no time
and occupies no space
in our companionship

that creates a heaven-sent gift,
as if we made a child;
though now it is our magnum opus
we will fashion out of Love.

Here is a change worth living for
and worthy of one's dying;
for grateful acceptance of mercy's will
weaves etheric light garments
that lift us up all the way
to other worlds.

Fare thee well, my dearest love;
I will see you in my dreams.

Stepping through the Veil
Love's Spirit offers her a vision of her twin flame

Intensely bright—you can hardly look
at the pure white radiance
spilling into your room.

A figure appears,
holding out a welcoming hand,
bidding you to step into the Light.

Will you accept the invitation?

Are you receptive enough
to face the eyes of your soul's twin,
focusing his care and compassion upon you,
loaning you the perfect understanding
of the one whose being you would know
with the fullness of your own.

Reach out now and take the hand
that beckons you beyond the barrier
that is not really there.

HER TWIN FLAME SPEAKS
Only in your mind
does separation exist;
only a fearful heart
prevents the union you desire.

Relax and let the moonlit path
gently guide your feet;

the way is paved in milky starlight,
reaching up to infinity.

Look for me in the luminescence
of a thousand spiral nebulae.

Dare to meet me where I am;
gaze into my eyes and tell me
the story of my love for you—
the one you never quite believed.

Behold that story now
as crossing eons of time,
countless disappointments
yet infinitely more hours
of love and laughter,
and deep communion
shared in joy-filled moments
of sublime affection.

Our souls are always
seeking that reunion,
the promise of Eternity,
the fleeting touch of immortality
that reaches out to you this night—

if only you will dream of me
and take the step
that no one can take for you.

Learning to Dance on the Bridge Between Worlds

He sails up to etheric realms.
She must overcome her sense of separation.
His passionate desire to connect makes it so,
and their congruence deepens.

*May you feel my love enfold you
and know me as the sanctuary
whose door is always open.*

Crossing Over from Earth
Visions of his transition & of the future

Under a golden dome
I felt my heart spinning,
blooming like a rose
in the center of my being,
the fiery core containing
all wisdom, all power, all love
I would ever know.

Waterfalls of rainbow substance
enveloped me
in the effervescent fountain
that blesses and heals all who pass
into this radiant Otherworld.

Castles of eternity did I enter,
each one a flame flower
surrounding a secret chamber:
my inner sanctum,
the holy of holies
where my True Self rests
in perpetual prayer.

An image of our oneness appeared,
an icon engraved on crystalline walls
as a surety of future bliss;
and I knew this place
as a bridal chamber
where one day you and I will be joined
for good, for joy, for hope, for unity.

I learned to abide
in the Light of my Presence,
centered, awake,
grounded, at peace;
becoming a lotus
floating on still waters,
a lily emanating purity's scent,
a ruby rose so exquisitely fragrant
that bees came to sip
the nectar of divine Love
that transformed my worldly strivings,
returning them to me as gifts of gold.

Basking in the golden-pink glow
that remains for me
both source and goal,
I felt unfolding out from my center
a pathway sprinkled with stardust,
illumined by an interior sun,
leading up to snow-capped peaks,
beckoning me to climb the summit,
fearless of its crags and chasms.

Yes! I cried, for I saw you
walking beside me in days to come,
our souls joined by a silver thread.

I felt you take my yearning to your breast
as your fervor came to me for safekeeping.

Earth to heaven, heaven to earth,
an exchange
we will make each day
in Spirit's Home,
where both of us
are whole in Love:
the reason for our being.

Beneath the golden dome
I beheld our souls spiraling
in galaxies of purest devotion,
welcoming pilgrims
who come to visit.

This is the service
we promised to undertake:
the essence of our future joy.

Galaxies
He describes the wonders of etheric realms

Whirling, spinning, spiraling,
bursting, scintillating,
projecting starry clusters
into deepest space.

These I have seen, beloved!
O, that I could bring you with me!

Rise with me that we might fly
beyond worlds,
to star systems
hurtling through space,
yet poised in perfect stillness,
focusing all their will
upon the fiery center
at the nucleus of all creation.

I am with you, my darling,
even as I am everywhere in cosmos.

Feel my passion burn in you
as soul recognizes soul once again
and reunion takes on new flavors of ecstasy.

Where you are, there am I also,
hidden in the deepest wellspring
of your holiness, the inner galaxy
whose starscape
you have only begun to explore.

Worlds await your presence, my darling.

Let my love carry you there;
for we have labors yet undone
and visions of grandeur to fulfill.

These are my prayers for you,
sweetest of hearts,
love of all my lifetimes.

Mystics gather, indeed,
in joyful anticipation
of words not yet spoken,
communion soon to be felt
and joy unbounded,
quivering in gratitude
for its imminent release,
as untold treasures of experience
are just ahead.

My darling,
let not your mind be anxious;
the path that leads
beyond the summit is not dark.

It bursts like fireworks
through veils of separation
into soul unities
where all is oneness:

essence to essence, galaxy to galaxy,
dancing for eternity
in the great T'ai Chi
of life becoming Life.

Step through the veil with me, beloved,
and come to know the glory
of your being and mine.

We are truly one
in the Love that is Reality.

I am the glow in your breast,
the warmth of tears that spring
in answer to my presence.

Swing wide the doors of consciousness
and see me standing before you;
feel me present with you
where I have always been.

Ten thousand lightyears are nothing
to the fullness of my love.

A Million Ways
She longs for his physical presence

After the rain you came to me
to dry my tears
and lift my soul
to dimensions of faith,
to help me believe in love
and hold me safe
as I had never been.

I still reach for you
in the night
to touch your invisible hand,
even as I feel
your spirit conjoined
with mine.

Deep is where I have to go
to reach you
and high above
where I had flown
before these days of loving.

Come find me again—
the weather has been stormy
and in those hours
I weary in walking.

Still, I hear your laughter
and need not look around
to know you stand beside me.

Separation is an illusion
that often feels real
until my body remembers
lying in your arms at night,
feeling the strength
of your spirit
and your will
to be my love forever—
even when I could not
hold you close enough
to keep you from
your destined path.

May my constancy
grow strong enough
to merit our reunion.

Eternity feels too small
for me to count
the million ways
I love you.

Equinox
He whispers to her a tender invitation

I come to you in joy
    like morning sun at springtime's dawn,
    a chickadee's song outside your window,
    the fragrance of hyacinths
    by the kitchen door,
    fresh coffee brewing on the stove.

I am the ground beneath your feet
    holding you up as you climb
    nearer and nearer to where I am.

Give your mind a rest, beloved;
    let thought drop deep within
    and then away into nothingness,
    for thoughts confuse
    when presence is what is needed
    here in this moment.

Run not hither and thither
    seeking other solutions
    when I am here
    with answers to questions
    you have not known to ask.

Our union is not linear;
    we dwell in a sphere where all is one
    in the circle of Love's embrace.

Relax, beloved;
    slip into timelessness with me
    and all will be revealed.

Be the poet of experience
    who leads by being;
    put away your books today
    and enter in where
    you have feared to go.

Meditate on your inner fire;
    let silence speak
    into your inner ear.

Be at peace and hear
    the springtime of my love.

Helping
He reassures her of his nearness

Beloved, listen carefully:
    Love is the answer
    to all your questions.

Expand the portals of perception,
    breathe in my devotion
    to your ascent,
    which is also mine;
    I am nearer than your breath,
    perhaps more vital
    to your journey Home.

Fly with me on violet wings;
    you are closer to being airborne
    than you realize,
    for your soul has been
    taking lessons in lifting off
    from earthly cares.

Spirit can create a magnet,
    as I proved some years ago;
    and now my heart burns
    with that same fire
    to bless and draw you
    all the way to where I am.

Come, join me in my sanctuary.

All in a Day
She experiences his presence with her

I felt you today, standing tall
where I fit right under your arm;
my body knew to nestle there,
safe—my soul joyfully greeting yours
like two children at recess.

Your gentle touch was strong
as an ancient oak,
backing me up,
overshadowing my trials,
seeing to my needs,
reassuring me of your closeness,
watching and participating
because I remembered
to invite you:
to help, to play, to advise,
to keep me anchored in reality.

Such is my way of life now—
now that I have accepted
that you have been here all along.

Only my ignorance prevailed,
blocking my view and spoiling the fun
we could have been having.

You do not blame me;
I feel that.

Somehow you know the reasons
better than I of why I resisted
and ran and pushed you away
along with all the holy blessings
I had long desired.

My mind is restless
and asks a lot of questions.

I pray that some of them
will contribute to the whole,
though few observers would believe it
to watch me wander and ponder
a thousand times a day.

Do you find me easier to love
from the heaven world?

Or did you always see
through the masks I wore
into the real person—hidden,
especially from myself?

Surely that is true.
You knew me from the beginning
and laid down your life
for me to finally
catch the vision.

Love of My Life
He helps her settle into their new reality

Love of my life, I see you
    as you have never seen yourself.

How could you not know—
    except we cannot behold
    our own brilliance
    unless another hold up a mirror
    of unwavering affection.

Beloved of my soul, you let me be myself—
    the greatest gift; for basking in your
    acceptance I learned to love even my
    frailties and shortcomings.

You, who are my other half,
    with you I am made whole,
    as with me you are also healed
    by promises kept
    and ancient puzzles solved.

Angel of my liberation,
    because of you, I come and go
    between the Here and Over There
    in harmony with your constancy.

United in this love that dissolves separation
    in Eternity's timelessness,
    I am forever and always yours:
    One. One. One. One.

Be still today, my love;
    the world is bathed in whiteness,
    stopped for a time in peacefulness.

May we, too, abide in silence,
    in deeper communion with each other,
    in meditation on life around us.

The rose of your heart is blooming.

What do you suppose real roses feel,
    growing new stems, making buds,
    reaching up for light and down for food;
    do they not strive to flower?

Nature works unceasingly
    to bear her fruits of being.

So must we also be true to mission;
    though our becoming
    is more complex,
    more perilous to manifest.

Come, lean upon me in my world;
    I will help you find your way.

Resist distraction today, my love;
    let me be the fullness
    of your experience.

The Presence
Her perception expands

Sitting with me
in the quiet of my room at midnight,
reassuring in its peaceful calm,
smiling upon me in profound compassion,
transmitting images
of more transcendent secrets
than the treasures I have discovered;

I feel the Presence coming nearer,
close enough to let me know
that fame and future do not matter,
for I am being joined
with my sweetheart
in the oneness I have longed to find.

I have felt this tender comfort
in times of deep connection
between my soul and my beloved's,
when our two hearts have sung together
in joy and laughter and in heartbreak.

We are ever joined by a silver thread:
Eternity's assurance that
no matter the travails we face
all is well with us
in realms of the unseen.

Thus life shall be in days to come;
and I will rejoice to carry
this Presence with me
for the remainder
of my sojourn here.

Though I walk on earthly pathways,
yet my delight is in the clouds,
my mind affixed on crystal bridges,
my hands reaching
up and out as Love directs.

Love is all there is,
and I am content
to follow where its Spirit leads.

When Grief Departs
After a time, she has an unexpected conversation

I am no longer your companion,
declared Grief one day—
an astonishing surprise to one
who had surrendered to heartache's
continuous company.

I have taught you all I can,
said Grief,
about perseverance
and your determination
to face me squarely,
look me in the eye
and forge a new life
through waves
of disappointment
and unavoidable sadness.

When those who mourn
learn my secrets,
I must depart.

And thus you have done—
plumbing my depths,
pushing back up from the bottom,
catching your breath,
then diving in again
to explore the dim waters
and dark caverns I hide from all
but the most intrepid swimmers.

Few know me as a Light force,
though I am the Divine's answer to loss
given before you dare to ask,
tucked away in your heart of hearts
against the day when Love
would break you open
(as it inevitably will)
and send you running
to the very core of all that is holy
in your True Self.

Oceanic am I,
and some think me cruel
in my stirring of
the body of sorrow.

Still, you found me out
and learned to surf my waves,
transmuting darkness into Light
in fires of creativity.

What am I, if not a flame—
agent of refiner's fire,
partner of my incandescent sister Joy,
who leaps out from your fractured heart
with golden gifts of pure insight,
forgiveness, gratitude and faith
that Love is ever
stronger than death.

I, Grief, bid you *adieu*;
my work is finished,
at least for now.

Should I appear at some later hour,
please welcome me as an honored guest,
for you will know what I am about
and I will trust you to fulfill
the spiral of our partnership.

And, lest you fear
to entertain me again,
Joy has promised to remind you
of her previous gifts
while she waits her turn
to brighten the day.

Few understand that we serve together,
though we always have and always will.

Linked by a Silver Thread
She learns to dance between worlds

I find myself awake, beloved!
And free at last to follow you
To Love's garden of spiritual delights
Where I have seen you in my dreams
Watching and praying that I would join you.

The power of your true love's magnet
Has called me over, across the bridge,
Through the gossamer veil of time
That for so long I dared not breach.

'Twas only fear that ruled my mind,
Though for what reason I am not sure;
Perhaps the skeptical voices of some
Who said I had to let you go.

I did let go, while you did not;
You kept me tethered to your spirit,
Sending messages across the wire
Of the delicate, silver filament
That has linked our souls since time began.

Your Home is beautiful, beloved;
O, that it could be also mine!
I promise I will win my place
As you earned yours through sacrifice
Of all you cherished in your life.

Meanwhile, I dance upon the bridge.

I close my eyes and see the way—
The golden, glistening, starlit path
That leads to where you wait for me

Near the crystalline healing fountain,
By an archway made of roses,
Yellow-pink and ruby-violet,
Whose fragrance permeates my being
Lifting me to where you are.

Though I feel you by my side,
I see now I must come to you,
Matching you in consciousness,
Sharing in your confidence
That I can reach up to the heavens.

In Light's awareness I must ascend
The mountain of adversity
That every climber must surmount
To greet her soul's twin in Love's garden.

I am here and over there,
Radiant in your sweet devotion,
Knowing you keep hold of me.

Our silver thread grows stronger now,
Shimmering in the bright starlight
That bursts aflame when twin souls meet.

Communing in the Ecstasy of Love Unbounded

*Twin flames pour out
the limitless fervor of their love
for each other
and for the Beloved.*

*In the sweetness of your devotion
I feel my True Self reflected.*

Sacred Embrace
Her twin flame calls her closer to himself

Breathe me in
as I breathe you out;
soul to soul
spirit to spirit
one in the same—
being in all being,
beloved transfigured
so beloved never dies.

Love me in you
as I love you in me;
my soul is yours—
you live in the center
of my body of Light
where I surrender
the secret of myself to you.

Touch your heart and feel my hand
clasping yours—tangible, real,
where you will always find me.

I am with you forever, my darling;
the radiance shining
out from you is also mine—
we are luminous being
in Eternity's kiss.

Love's Persons
A revelation from the Spirit of Love

I am Love.
Essence of the Divine.

Listen for my voices
in the peace
of your meditations.
I speak as persons
and cosmic forces.

Think of me as a flying carpet
or a winged horse
carrying lovers aloft
on their life's
greatest adventures.

Guiding, nurturing,
inspiring, chastising.

All of these are my roles
on behalf of yearning souls
who long to find themselves
enfolded in my Presence,
forever buoyed
by compassion's
nourishing waters,
subsumed in the blissful fires
of transfiguration.

Intention counts toward blessings
for travelers who expect miracles
while leaning their devotion
toward the Divine,
in confidence that
Love's will does prevail
for those who welcome
both fair and stormy weather.

May all who cherish connection
learn the wisdom
of a grateful demeanor.

I am Love.
Come closer now
and know me as the One
who brought you back together.

Contact
He greets her from beyond the veil

You will know we have connected
when tears come;
the tears that tell true,
dissolving separation
in an instant.

Doubt cannot enter here
and nothing bad ever happened
when you are at my side,
my darling.

The fire of my affection burns
like a precious chest wound,
singing of Home and oceans of Love
whose waves lap the shore
of my soul, chanting:
We are one.
We are one.
We are one.

Come, sit with me awhile, beloved,
and learn a secret:

Eternity is a hologram,
a glistening, swirling blue bauble
held in the palm of Spirit's hand,
where contact goes on forever
in the flow of smiles and tears
and ineffable joy.

Recollection
A memory, long forgotten, occurs to her

I saw you once
    in another life,
        a celebrated man
        of letters and of poetry;
        and thought you were a god.

Laurel-crowned
    as in Roman times
    you appeared—
        my imagination
        conjuring liminal scenes
        while seated at
        a simple dinner party.

Did you notice me, perchance?

A poet, young, with miles to go,
while yours were running out.

Remembering now,
    'twas long ago;
    yet, how could I have
        forgot the spark
        when you turned,
        just so, and looked—
        as from a lofty height,
        down centuries into my soul.

Your eyes held mine for a mere instant,
    though long enough
    to flash the slightest of smiles
    and a clear promise:

    "Not now," your eyes said;
    "but soon, as Eternity counts time,
    when stars align with
    the Divine's desires.

    "Save a verse for me, beloved,
    and I will meet you in the garden."

We Will Always Have Roses
The vow he makes to her before every embodiment

We will always have roses
spring, winter or fall.

And Midsummer, especially,
brings blossoms that call
from the best of the garden's
bright festival display:
"Gather pink for your sweetheart,
and do not delay."

I will always have roses
alive in my heart
when I think of you, darling,
and how precious thou art
to me now and forever.

My love will not wane
whether we are together
or separate again.

For our souls are joined
like two buds on a stem;
we spring from one plant
though we bloom in strange lands.

Our missions may differ
and take us afar
from each other for purposes
larger than we are.

Still, you are flesh of my flesh
and bone of my bone;
with you I am made whole
and never alone.

I carry your love
in the heart of my heart,
remembering always
that I am a part
of your soul's very fabric,
as you are of mine.

We are woven together
till the end of all time.

There will always be roses
where you are concerned;
my love is not seasonal
and need not be earned.

Our bond is eternal,
and there lies my faith
that we will stay young forever
like two buds in a vase.

Duet
They sing an ecstatic love song

SHE

> We are not who we were,
> and step by step
> we are becoming more
> of who we really are.

HE

> Gifts long tucked away
> are emerging, peaking out
> like children in their pj's,
> rubbing their eyes awake
> after a long sleep.

SHE

> Facets of self,
> forgotten in ages
> of distraction and confusion,
> are now being polished
> to mirror sheen
> by one another's
> adoring attention.

HE

My love calls out these gems in you
and your love beckons
what is most real in me,
to honor, to cherish,
to nurture and uphold,
to champion and manifest
dreams believed impossible
in the dimness of forgetfulness.

SHE
>	We shine, beloved,
> in the radiance of mutual gratitude;
> two candles touching
> an incandescent infinity.

HE
>	I pour the fullness of my being
> into the waiting chalice
> of your acceptance, in faith
> that your love flows back to me,
> while waves of your devotion
> caress the shore of all that I am,
> body, spirit, mind and soul.

SHE
>	The ocean of my love
> knows no limits in the antiphon
> of emptying and filling.

HE
>	I become a world in order
> to contain the precious exchange
> of my life for yours and yours for mine,
> until we are only waves of Light,
> rushing to each other
> in the exhilaration
> of Love's sweet alchemy
> of giving and receiving
> that changes us forever into
> the eternal unity of the Beloved.

Surrounded in Love
He rejoices in her nearness

So perfectly joined are our two souls
that distance is a thing of the past
and separation an event that never happened.

My love for you exceeds the mountain heights
where we have sat beside crystal-clear waters
in blissful contemplation.

And yet so perfectly contained am I
in your heart that I am compressed
as a tiny ruby, relishing the many facets
of my affection and regard.

You are meeting me at last, my darling,
at Home, where I have always been,
waiting for you to realize
the fullness of my love.

The pleasure of your company shines
as luminous starlight, and I bask
in the radiance of your affirmation
of all that is fine and holy between us.

Time slips by on silent sands, and heaven
permeates your dwelling place and mine.

We are one as we were always meant to be;
and I rejoice that now you know
with your whole body, mind and spirit
the truth of our indelible bond.

The Meeting Place
Twin flames affirm their togetherness

S<small>HE SPEAKS FIRST</small>

>Here in a crystalline chamber
>>we come together;
>>two separates no longer,
>>now a single whole
>>in this place of serenity
>>>where you found you
>>>and I found me
>>>in the mirror
>>>of our oneness,
>>>>the image
>>>>of our origin.

>We pray through that icon
>>as through an open door,
>>a picture window
>>that opens out
>>to glory upon glory,
>>>limitless expansiveness
>>>borne on a soft breeze
>>>meant to keep us moving,
>>>>our hearts spinning
>>>>in the pure joy
>>>>of being together
>>>>in our soul essence.

H E RESPONDS

    I see you now, resplendent,
        as a blossom in a field
        of yellow lilies so perfect
            you cannot be other
            than the fragrance
            that breathes into you
                as your lily-self
                tucks her feet
                into the soil
                    and sways
                    her head
                    this way
                    and that,
                    intent on
                    attracting bees.

A Blanket of Comfort for the Soul
Insight from the Beloved

The rose of your heart
has been there all along,
opening out in a spiral
all the way to the secret center,
the holiest of holies.

None can know the contact
another makes
with all-consuming Love
whose feeling in the breast
is cool as peppermint heat—

penetrating, expanding,
piercing and emanating,
glowing and growing,
enveloping and consuming
all unlike itself.

Touch now with all your senses
the point of sublime contact:
soft as baby's breath,
a blanket of comfort for the soul,

a brilliant ray of crystal-pink Light
that opens a portal
to the core of your being
in the serene stillness
of the perfectly balanced
spinning of the heart center
in deep meditation.

These Days, Celebrate
Her twin speaks from a full heart

Now is the time for love.
These days are meant for love.
Let's get caught up in the moment;
No thought about somewhere in time
When life meant or will mean more.

Let now be the moment
That steals the breath away.
    And let's fill that pause
    With the recognition
        That we are two souls
        Sharing life.

Today. Now. We smell the roses.
Let's be that rose,
    Perfect in every moment
    Of its existence.

No, let's be more than that rose.
    Let's celebrate in the awareness
    Of our essence and the knowledge
        That we, that you
        Will be a part of me
        Forever.

Come, celebrate these days
With me, beloved.
    We have never had
    More cause to rejoice
    Than today.

Return to Innocence
She reflects upon their journey through Love

Sweet as young life,
childlike we have become.

Somehow, impervious
to the wiles of serpents,
we laugh in their faces,
not in derision (that is their game),
but in amusement at their machinations
and then, of course, in sadness
that they should turn their backs
on a divine Love so freely given.

Is this innocence,
this lack of complication,
where we came from?

We certainly are not gullible.
Our eyes are wide open
in wonder and discernment
like those little ones
who saw through
the emperor's lack of clothing,
remarking in their guilelessness
on the naked truth before them.

Ourselves, we are not young—
merely drawn closer in heavenly realms
by Love and only Love
as the subject of our allegiance
and our way of being together.

We see each other's souls, beloved;
and in that seeing, we become
as children in one another's eyes,
worthy of the tenderest care
and yet desirous of correction.

Children, in their souls,
long for a parent's guiding hand,
which we offer to each other;
and in that giving we pull the two of us
up to more refined togetherness.

We did not expect to find innocence;
power, light, wisdom—yes, all of these.

Yet, strolling in Love's garden
we come to understand
the source of all these gifts
is the sweetness of pure perception
that does not taint what it perceives.

Rather, we strive to raise
all life around us
so friends and strangers
might also be transformed.

And thus resolved,
we take the next step into transfiguration
and feel the whole world fill up
with light and joy.

Living Life to the Full

*Twin flames savor every aspect
of their oneness
as they give their all
to the Beloved.*

*May your presence be a promise fulfilled,
a prayer answered,
a kindness spontaneous
in its expression.*

A Promise
The Spirit of Love reveals its essence

Love is a promise to be faithful
to a holy vow

To live in integrity,
to right any wrongs,
to make things better

To fix the broken,
mend the torn,
heal the wounded

Smooth the jagged edges,
repair what has been damaged,
fill up empty hearts

All with Love,
for the sake of Love,
for the future of Love

In order that Love
may continue unfettered,
picking up dropped stitches,
retrieving bits of soul
you have left strewn
along life's path.

Each act of Love
is a promise fulfilled
and a promise
to act again for Love.

Love cannot be separated from itself;
wherever its exists,
completeness is found.

Love is never partial,
being singularly
and eternally aware
only of wholeness.

Such is Love's bountiful nature
that it reaches out
to multiply its essence
wherever life has need
of succor and relief.

This is how Love works;
I promise.

What We Do for Love
Twin flames reach out in tender care

SHE

    I place my resistances
on the altar of your wisdom
    so all my foibles may be found out,
    my vulnerabilities revealed,
        my shortcomings dissolved
        in the mercy of your love for me.

HE

    I place my faith in your compassion
and trust you do the same for me;
    once we name our imperfections
    and shake them like dust
    from the folds of our garments,
        we cry "a-ha!"
        when they appear again
           and banish them
           from consciousness.

SHE

    Relinquishing fear is our glad sacrifice,
    while those who live in doubt
    shudder to give up their defenses;
        malleable we would become,
        willing to be Spirit-led,
        happy in humility,
           surrendering ourselves
           to Love's bright way
                as we forgive, forgive
                and continue to forgive.

HE
    I find myself forgetting me;
    a certain smallness drops away
        and largesse opens
        my awareness
            in deep concern
            for you, beloved.

SHE
    I overflow with love and care
    my only desire to serve and serve,
        to pour the abundance
        of my True Self
        into the chalice
        of your sweet heart,
            even as I lift
            my emptied cup
            to receive the elixir
            of your devotion.

HE
    This we do for one another,
    on behalf of all who cross our paths;
        each day a ritual of passage
        as Love accepts
        our humble gifts
            and turns them
            into Spirit's gold.

My Brother
Watching his older sibling in his backyard

Nearly twins, so close in age were we;
different in temperament,
many days more competitors than friends,
yet brothers all the way.

Defenders of one another's territory,
champions of each other's choices
that we often strained to understand.

You stayed for family;
I took off chasing rainbows,
reaching for the seemingly unattainable.

Are we more alike now?
Both of us broken open,
cracked so the Light of Love could shine
through from unexpected sources?

Watching you today, I see for the first time
we were both born to be householders,
and how unique each one's path became.

You stayed long enough
for new family to come to you.

I left too soon, or perhaps right on time,
when rainbows called,
pointing me toward the sun
where my heart filled up with the love
that I am sending to you today, my brother.

Acknowledging What Is
Insight from the Beloved

Love remains when all is taken from you,
    even your identity as half of a pair
    that alters when one must leave
    and one must surrender to thriving.

Not hiding, but embracing the life
    that, for a time, insists on pulling you
    away from your heart's desire.

That proves how strong you are,
    resilient and able to let go
    your sense of separation,
    to learn that both of you are whole,
    each of you complete,
    in the world where you abide.

Two wholes make a totality;
    not merely a gathering of pieces,
    but a new reality arising
    when you two become one
    and know yourselves in none other,
    as you speak with a voice that sounds
    of quiet melodies sung in sweet unison:

A single note that birthed you
    in the beginning when you
    embraced new earthly existence
    and set out on this adventure
    to prove that Love lives on forever
    for those who yearn to believe 'tis so.

At Home in Love's Garden
She pours out her love to her twin soul

Beloved of my eternal life!
How often have we walked
these soft green paths,
marveling in delight
at Nature's sheer abundance.

Sweet birdsong wafts gaily
through flowering trees,
while myriad plants and animals
flourish in this liminal realm
that holds our worlds together.

My heart-fire glows, warming my body;
my love is transformed by loving you
without limit or hesitation.

Your hand strong in mine is the surety
that we may live as Nature does
in giving and receiving the devotion
that grows between and in us,
nurtured in this sun-lit atmosphere.

Wisdom's deep knowing
pervades our radiant garden,
expanding vibrant consciousness.

Here we know each other truly
as if a thousand lifetimes
had never intervened since our beginning,

and holiness had always been
the fragrance of our thoughts
and words and deeds.

Forgiveness enfolds us, beloved;
and every flower in the garden
blooms in transmutation's
healing ways.

Only mercy is present here,
beaming through a generous Spirit
who minds our present and our past
so we might be forever transformed.

Womb-like, the garden carries us,
creating a new oneness out of two,
till we emerge in harmony—
able, at last, to call this Home
the foundation of our future work:

Love in service of transfiguration,
transfiguration in the service
of eternal Love.

Lean on Faith
He encourages her to persevere

Have faith in your invincible True Self
and let that Faith
be a personal presence
to anchor you in practical work
that I would do for both of us
if I were yet alive on earth.

Trust in Faith's constancy
when she offers you
the blessing of herself.

Faith is a mother
who sustains your path
when all seems lost in dark nights
and seasons of regret.

She knows the yearning of your heart,
the sighing of your soul
in longing for a taste
of Love's transfiguring power.

Faith is true-blue
in moments of extremity,
a stalwart champion
of your desire to burn
with reunion's fires
of unquenchable delight.

She holds an unwavering vision,
an optimistic certainty
of your arrival at that holy place
where twin souls find
the fullness of themselves
reflected in the wholeness
of each other.

Faith wields the strength
of a sword of Truth
as she clears the way
for travelers to conquer
the roughest mountains of adversity.

She stays the night to banish doubt
and lends the wounded heart
her confidence that even in the midst
of Love's chastisements
the Beloved is always true
and will not fail to long endure.

Faith's blessing is incorruptible
in the fidelity of her Presence
and the steadfastness of her Love.

Lean on Faith
and she will see you Home.

Hope's Gift of Renewal
Twin flames joyfully speak as with a single voice

Hope flew in on starlight;
a gift of renewal,
energy and joyful anticipation
of adventures yet to come—

the stuff of dreams,
promises of love and faith
that the best of our intentions
will bear fruit.

Somehow with hopeful hearts
it matters less that futures are invisible
as travelers we go map-less
into the dark,
trusting we will find a lamp,
the moon will rise and daylight
will remain inevitable.

Hope is a grace that tells us
we are mission-born,
endowed with native worthiness
possessed of gifts unique and fine,
cherished by Spirit for our Self,
each one a gem in Beauty's crown.

There is a plenitude in Hope
that fosters generous connection,
encouraging us to reach out

to those we know and others
we have not met till now,
to connect with land
and sea and sky
and all the creatures
that call them home.

In Hope we feel ourselves
at one with life,
believing it will always be thus,
until an ill wind
blows coldly through

closing our minds
to what might be,
engendering fear,
causing us to lose
the precious gift of Hope.

Like a child or pet or plant,
Hope must be nourished,
watered and fed.

A myth exists that one needs Hope
to open up compassion to life;
but, truly, it is the open heart
that magnetizes Hope's mercy
with gratitude and loving-kindness.

Hope stays for Joy,
grows strong in Faith,
builds scaffolds of positive regard
and longs to be at Home
with practical souls
who will not lose her from neglect.

Hope illuminates the evening sky
with starlight
born of pilgrims' prayers
and wishes for a better world
sent up to heaven
by humble hearts

so that Hope may then
return to earth
to lift the weight
from those who toil,
yet even in their darkest hours
can still say, *Yes!*
when Spirit calls.

Love in Action
An unexpected presence appears

Charity, they call me, though few perceive
My nature in the modern sense;
Thinking me, perhaps, to be acting
Out of guilt or regret, salving
My own wounds with hand-me-downs
In a show of beneficence
To the poor, down-trodden masses.

How sad! How untrue!
I give my best and gladly, fervently,
Exuberantly, from the depths of my being
To anyone in need of Love.
And who is not in need, these days?

I am the very essence of Love.
My nature is to shower my abundance
On the whole universe—
Indeed, an entire cosmos is too small
To contain my passion for spreading
My love into barren places of arid souls,
Inspiring those deserts to bloom.

Excuse me, please, I cannot tarry.
A world calls for healing;
And I am there this instant,
Laying down the very substance of myself,
So twin flames who would be whole
May live another day to learn
And give back Love to life in action
The way I, Charity, have loved them.

Life Lived to the Full
His dialogue with the Spirit of Love

HE POSITS
> Some well may ask—
> How is a life lived to the full
> when one no longer exists on earth
> in a physical body that can be seen?
>
> I ask in turn—
> Can life be lived to full abundance
> when the soul abides for a time in clay,
> an earthly house of limitation?

LOVE'S SPIRIT ANSWERS
> 'Tis both and each.
> You fill the vessel you are given
>> with all the love you can muster,
>> reaching ever in and upward
>> to your True Self in realms of Light,
>> always outward to your twin soul
>> who carries on for both of you
>> in daily rounds of serving life.
>
> Souls in love move back and forth
>> whether in or out of human form
>> bringing more of divinity to earth
>> perfecting the chalice of flesh
>> to contain more light, love and joy,
>> for true love's sake and for the sake
>> of those bright twins
>> who will surely follow after you.

Grounded in Glory
She rejoices in their wholeness

My beloved, we have turned
    a cosmic corner;
        this clay no longer limits me.

I feel a grounded sense of being
    transcending even the poetry
    of our contemplation.

Words fail in the midst of this glory.

Here is true harmony of oneness;
    puzzle pieces in place,
    locked together for eternity
    in the completed image.

My darling, whosoever sees me
    sees you, and wonders not
    to perceive two in one,
    for only one is visible.

I feel my wholeness
    as I rest in you
    and you abide in me,
    in solid there-ness
    that may be inexplicable
    except to those
    who are blessed
    with gazing
    beyond clay eyes.

The Heart of the Matter
Twin flames reflect on their journey

We sojourn through the nucleus:
    portal of far-off worlds
    gateway to Presence
    realm of our reflection
    the very center of existence
        where stars are born
        and galaxies spiral
        in eternal majesty.

Our reason for being
    abides in the heart,
    secreted away
    in its inner chamber,
        where lovers meet in purity,
        each one uniquely unified,
        male and female balanced
        in delicate equipoise.

We join our singleness of being
    with our lover's centered wholeness,
    never more to venture away,
    Home at last where we began
    though wiser now, compassionate,
    filled with soul-gifts freely given,
        the fruit of our most holy vow
        in promises remembered
        and fulfilled.

Transfiguration is a pathless path
    awakened ones will come to know
    by gratefully giving of themselves.

We have loved our way
    through transmutation,
    entering now a secret chamber
    whose door swings wide
    in the radiant gratitude
    of reunion's blissful effervescence,
        the gold of True Love's alchemy
        distilled by the refiner's fires
        till Light and only Light remains
            where Faith with Hope
            and Joy abide together
            in Spirit's perfect peace.

Sparkling Like Diamonds

*Twin flames rejoice in the
ineffable beauty of their union.
Love commissions them to share
their oneness with other souls
who yearn for the Beloved.*

*May spirals of joy flow in & around you
as you bask in the sublime wholeness
of harmony with your twin flame.*

The Best Days of Our Lives
His love for her overflows in ecstasy

O, my great love!
These are the best days
of our many lives,
though not the easiest by far.

Every day the veil must part
by prayer and devotion's
sweet attunement
over the filigree thread
of heart connection

through the latticework
of elevated thought,
in the deep quiet
of living peace

with faith that whom
Spirit has joined none can part
when love prevails
in all our striving
for transfiguration.

We meet as in
a bridal chamber,
a place of holy consummation,
where soul to soul
we affirm our bond;
beloved to beloved
we surrender all.

Hand in hand
we walk our path
to share our love
with a troubled world
in need of hope that daily life
is luminous,
at times miraculous,
when step by step
Love's Spirit leads.

My life is full
as I see you there,
doing our sacred labor on earth
while I work for us
in heavenly realms.

Forgiveness reigns
o'er all our days
in a never-ending
flow of love,
for only good things
ever happened,
and a beautiful joy
is our reward.

Antiphon of Rejoicing
They call & answer in mutual exultation

Joy arrives,
simply, suddenly,
as if delivered by an unseen hand.

We do not find Joy;
she finds us
and changes us forever.

Once touched by Joy,
we are never satisfied with less;
she is of the Divine,
a quality of soul,
a reminder of our origin.

Joy is a catalyst for connection,
compassion and delight
that amplify her luminance
so we may beam
her spirit to others.

When Joy fills us up
with her perfect essence,
we feel whole, complete
and ecstatically real.

Joy lands where she will and joins us
to her effervescent flow
that banishes all sense
of separation.

Even in poignant circumstance,
when Spirit comes
to sit with us,
our eyes fill up with joyful tears;
and we know in our souls
we are not bereft,
for Joy has made
her presence known.

Joy is not of this world,
though she attends our important rites
of human passage—
a touch of heavenly celebration
when we transcend a difficult past
and wake up to a holy instant.

Joy is present when souls are born,
and at the end of their days
she leads them Home and thins the veil
for those who would see,
offering a glimpse of life's bookends
that she waits upon so faithfully.

We may resist the call of Joy.

Something in us knows
she comes at a cost
that many saints have dearly paid

as angel arrows pierced their hearts
with a living flame of Love that burned
then quickly filled them up
with its unfathomable joy.

Dare we answer such a call?

We, whom Joy has graciously touched,
will answer, *Yes!*
when she beckons us;
for we have come to know her
as Spirit's reward for stepping off
into the Unknown,
embracing life's great challenges.

In times of sublime connection
with Joy's indescribable *something*,
she seems to lend us
a surge of courage,
the fire of her sisters Faith and Hope,
in exhilarating realization
that we are made of joyful stuff.

And in those moments
our burning hearts confirm
that we are one
with Love's alchemical power
that transfigures us into itself.

In an Orb of Love's Pure Radiance
Love's Spirit observes twin souls in their sphere

Delicate as a soap bubble is their orb,
    scintillating as pure diamond crystals
    shimmering in the noonday sun,

Transparent as rose-pink glass
    and round as an orange,
    a sphere of iridescent Light,
    reflecting rainbows
    on its surface as it turns,

They will only see it from the inside;
    it abides deep within them
    as a tiny flame of clarity
    that grows to encompass their bodies,
    to fill the room where they have
    invited the Light of Love to settle in,
    to stay and bless the space.

One does not journey to this sphere.

The only movement is of the heart
    beating in consonance with the twin,
    the perfect partner of her soul,
    the tinder for his spark
    that will ignite for good
    when both of them are complete,
    male and female in each one.

Their orb is of the air,
    yet solid as earth, fluid as water,
    and able to withstand the heat
    of the refiner's fire.

Gentle as a womb, strong as a fortress
    with room for only two
    who would be one again,
    as they were in the beginning,
    and have not been for eons.

They form the orb out of themselves,
    creating a cocoon to nestle in,
    impervious to the outside world,
    in remembrance of their origin
    when time began for them
    in a starry nursery—as a single sphere
    that had not yet been twinned,
    spinning them out to love the world
    back to their Father/Mother God.

Today the orb's inhabitants look out upon
    the earth with compassionate smiles,
    as parents often marvel at the
    antics of their noisy children
    who seem oblivious
    to their watchfulness.

Only those in other orbs
    detect the presence of these two
    in the reality of their ensconced form,
    created of Love's essence.

Tissue-thin it is, and strong as armor,
    clear as holiday twinkle lights,
    self-illumining, filled with
    life-giving energy
    to nourish and protect the pair
    for as long as their love shall live.

In ages past they found it difficult
    to remain within the orb;
    obligations and distractions
    called them out until
    their sphere dissolved away,
    leaving them to wonder what
    was missing from their intimacy.

Nowadays, in their orb once more,
    they meet on a bridge
    between two worlds
    to pass their messages back and forth
    like couriers connected by a silver thread
    that stretches and contracts
    with the work at hand.

One day they stop on their crystalline span
    and hand each other a simple note;
    they stand and read,
    and then they smile,
    as their roseate orb
    intensifies about them.

The message is a simple one:
    Whom Love has joined
    let nothing split
    by subterfuge or insinuation;
    you belong to one another,
    never more to go astray.

They embrace again in gratitude
    and disappear into their orb,
    sailing for a time to golden heavens,
    soon to return in joyful service
    toward all the waiting beings
    that I, Love, send them off to aid.

The Key that Opens the Door

*When souls are grateful,
Love's kindness & joy flow abundantly
in fulfillment of sacred purpose.*

*May your quest for reunion
with your twin flame
bring you eternal blessings
from the heart of Love's Spirit.*

Accepting the Gift of Transfiguration
A request from the Spirit of Love

In the golden-pink glow of a radiant dawn
I come to greet you once again,
you and your beloved twin
whose souls I cherish beyond your dreams.

Though perhaps you do not recall,
I have been with you both since time began,
when you were first formed from starry substance,
a twinkle in the firmament,
destined to find your way to earth
to forge a path back to my heart.

When you feel the heat of my regard
as discipline or chastisement,
please receive me with gratitude;
all my striving is for your sake,
that you might become once more like stars,
brilliant, shining as your True Self,
now unified with one another
in the wholeness each one has gained.

My flames work with delicate precision,
melting burdens that have held you back
from the bliss of companionship with your twin flame.

Please meet me with courage, accept my gift;
your hearts know the way to reunion
comes through the fire of transfiguration
that is, to your souls, Love's ultimate kindness—
the key that opens the door to joy.

Our Hearts Overflow with Gratitude
in the presence of the Beloved

After my Stephen's departure for etheric realms, he beamed back to me his ecstatic declaration, "There is joy in heaven!"

With the publication of these stories, poems and meditations that have emerged from the most intimate depths of our hearts, I can truly say, "There is joy on earth!"

Our Gratitude Abounds

We wish to express our heartfelt thanks to our colleagues, Theresa McNicholas, James Bennett and Paula Kehoe, for your steady dedication to excellence in all aspects of our endeavors. We share a passion for creating works of art and chalices for the Word, which is a profound joy.

Stephen and I are also very grateful to our family and friends who have held us close in all our strivings.

Our deepest gratitude goes to the great Wisdom Teachers whose kindness brought us together in this life. These generous masters have walked with us through our many trials of mortality and continue to guide and guard us in more ways that we can count.

We are beyond grateful for the opportunity they have given us to share our small part of the universal, transfiguring drama of twin flames in Love.

To you who are reading our words, we extend our sincere appreciation for your willingness to join us on this journey. May we all continue to support and encourage one another as we follow our hearts wherever the Beloved leads.

Love is the way and Joy paves the path with roses.

Cheryl Lafferty Eckl with Stephen Alan Eckl

*May you see reflected in the glass
the face of Love, the understanding heart,
the countenance of joy & peace
that shines forth from the Beloved's smile,
returning to you the blessing
of each compassionate word & tender service
you have ever offered along life's way.*

Cheryl Lafferty Eckl is an award-winning author, mystical poetess and storyteller.

A long-time student of the spiritual paths of East & West, she holds a master's certificate in Transpersonal Psychology, and is passionate about helping others achieve reunion with their own True Self.

Cheryl lives in Montana, where the rarefied atmosphere of Big Sky Country inspires her to pay deep attention to the promptings of the Beloved—to learn and grow, and then share those insights with others.

Learn more at www.CherylEckl.com.

www.ingramcontent.com/pod-product-compliance
Lightning Source LLC
Chambersburg PA
CBHW020425010526
44118CB00010B/433